REALMS OF LIGHT

PHOTOGRAPHS BY ERNST HAAS

A COLLECTION OF POETRY THROUGH THE AGES

EDITED BY SAMUEL S. WALKER, JR.

WALKER AND COMPANY   720 FIFTH AVENUE   NEW YORK, NEW YORK 10019

ABOUT ERNST HAAS

Ernst Haas, acclaimed as one of the most celebrated and influential photographers of the century, was born in Vienna, Austria, in 1921. He attended medical school, but his strong artistic bent led him to the camera. In 1947 his first exhibit was held in Vienna. In 1949 Haas joined the cooperative agency MAGNUM and launched his memorable ''Returning Prisoners Of War'' photo essay.

Since he came to the United States in 1951, one-man exhibits of his work have been held at the Museum of Modern Art, Asia House, The IBM Gallery, Rizzoli Gallery, The International Center Of Photography, The Museum of The Twentieth Century (Vienna) and The Photokina Center (Cologne) on three different occasions. Haas has received numerous awards, including the Newhouse Award, ASMP's Honor Roll and the Kulturpreis (Germany).

Haas wrote, directed and narrated a series of four programs titled *The Art Of Seeing,* which were aired on NET-TV in 1962. Among his many film assignments have been *The Misfits, Moby Dick, West Side Story* and *Little Big Man,* and he was consultant to John Houston on the film *The Bible* for the first segment on the creation.

He is the author of *The Creation, In America, In Germany* and *Himalayan Pilgrimage,* and has contributed to many other photographic books.

series editor: Samuel S. Walker, Jr.
art director: Judith Woracek
research: Peter T. Starr
managing editor: Andrea H. Curley
production: David Kellogg

The Editor gratefully acknowledges the assistance of Marina Filicori and Marilyn Schroeder.

ISBN: 0-8027-0619-3   Library of Congress Catalog Card Number: 78-59794

Printed in the United States of America   10   9   8   7   6   5   4   3   2   1

ACKNOWLEDGMENTS AND COPYRIGHT NOTICES

The Editors wish to thank the following for permission to reprint the poems listed:

The Belknap Press of Harvard University Press. ''A Light Exists.'' Reprinted by permission of the publishers and the Trustees of Amherst College from *The Poems of Emily Dickinson,* edited by Thomas E. Johnson, Cambridge, Mass.: The Belknap Press of Harvard University Press © 1951, 1957 by the President and Fellows of Harvard College.

Montcalm Productions. ''August Rainbows.'' Copyright © 1974 by Montcalm Productions, written by Rod McKuen.

Delacorte Press. ''Afterglow.'' From *Selected Poems 1923-1967* by Jorge Luis Borges, translated by Norman Thomas DiGiovanni, Copyright © 1968, 1969, 1971 by Jorge Luis Borges. Originally appeared in *The New Yorker.* Used by permission of Delacorte Press/Seymour Lawrence.

Doubleday & Company. Excerpt from *Diary of a Young Girl* by Anne Frank. Copyright 1952 by Otto H. Frank.

David R. Godine, Publisher. From ''Autumn Shade'' in *Living Together: New and Selected Poems* by Edgar Bowers. © 1956, 1965, 1973.   PAGE 107 CONSTITUTES AN EXTENSION OF THIS COPYRIGHT PAGE.

CONTENTS

EDITOR'S FOREWORD

Men have written about Light since Ikhnaton's *Hymn to the Sun* (c. 1365 B.C.) and probably long before. Light has been equated with Life and the Deity in every civilization, primitive and modern. Scientists, loath to admit mystification, cannot fully describe or explain this form of energy, its ultimate source or its properties (does it have weight? is it a wave or a particle?). Poets and artists have been more successful, partly because none has presumed to offer a *total* explanation, content to cast a slanting ray on a particular moment.

This book is a collection of such moments, visual and verbal. Each poem and each photograph has been selected because it has something significant to add to our understanding of the subject, sometimes awesome, sometimes gently humorous. It is best to read this book slowly, as one sips a fine wine, savoring each taste. Allow the words and images to swirl together and interact in your mind. Consider yourself an artist picking from the shapes and forms and colors on your palette to create a new, very personal masterpiece.

There is no contrived relationship between the words and photographs; one is not intended to *illustrate* the other. The association is casual, free, almost accidental, as when two friends meet unexpectedly. Each has an individual life independent of the other, but they get along well together and enrich one another.

Darkness exists only as the *absence* of Light, as cold is the absence of heat and death the absence of life. While white is a combination of all colors, black is the absence of any. Blackness, cold, death—the Void—are negative expressions of absences, while Light is the supreme symbol of the positive, the Good.

Have you ever thought how little it takes, the merest pinpoint of light, to dispel the darkness?

How little we understand! We can't see light (only its source and its reflection; the light itself is invisible), and we can't see without it. We share the quandry with C. S. Lewis whose Robin, in *The Man Born Blind*, after gaining sight for the first time, asks:

"...where is the light itself? You see you won't say. Nobody will say. You tell me the light is here and the light is there, and this is in the light and that is in the light, and yesterday you told me I was in your light, and now you say that light is a bit of yellow wire in a glass bulb hanging from the ceiling. Call that light? Is that what Milton was talking about? If you don't know what light is, why can't you say so?"

We can answer better, perhaps, after dwelling on the images which follow.

S.S.W.

from MEMORIES, DREAMS, REFLECTIONS

At that time I understood that within the soul from its primordial beginnings there has been a desire for light and an irrepressible urge to rise out of the primal darkness. When the great night comes, everything takes on a note of deep dejection, and every soul is seized by an inexpressible longing for light. That is the pent-up feeling that can be detected in the eyes of primitives, and also in the eyes of animals. There is a sadness in animals' eyes, and we never know whether that sadness is bound up with the soul of the animal or is a poignant message which speaks to us out of that still unconscious existence. That sadness also reflects the mood of Africa, the experience of its solitudes. It is a maternal mystery, this primordial darkness. That is why the sun's birth in the morning strikes the natives as so overwhelmingly meaningful. The *moment* in which light comes *is* God. That moment brings redemption, release.

CARL JUNG

light, a form of energy the nature of which is not yet satisfactorily established.

THE COLUMBIA ENCYCLOPEDIA

from DEJECTION: AN ODE

A Light, a Glory, and a luminous Cloud
Enveloping the Earth!

SAMUEL TAYLOR COLERIDGE

[6]

IMPRESSIONIST PICTURE OF A GARDEN

Give me sunlight, cupped in a paint brush,
And smear the red of peonies
Over my garden.
Splash blue upon it,
The hard blue of Canterbury bells,
Paling through larkspur
Into heliotrope,
To wash away among forget-me-nots
Dip red again to mix a purple,
And lay on pointed flares of lilacs against bright green.
Streak yellow for nasturtiums and marsh marigolds
And flame it up to orange for my lilies.
Now dot it so—and so—along an edge
Of Iceland poppies.
Swirl it a bit, and faintly,
That is honeysuckle.
Now put a band of brutal, bleeding crimson
And tail it off to pink, to give the roses.
And while you're loaded up with pink,
Just blotch about that bed of phlox.
Fill up with cobalt and dash in a sky
As hot and heavy as you can make it;
Then tree-green pulled up into that
Gives a fine jolt of colour.
Strain it out,
And melt your twigs into the cobalt sky.
Toss on some Chinese white to flash the clouds,
And trust the sunlight you've got in your paint.
There is the picture.

AMY LOWELL

The eye's light is a noble gift of heaven. All beings live from light, each
fair created thing, the very plants, turn with a joyful transport to the
light.

FRIEDERICH VON SCHILLER

T THE LIGHT TOLD ME

w a circle, now a spiral or wheel.

ges with the eye, with a wing or a sickle-shaped horn.

s on the form of beasts—a dragon, fish or bird.

orb, at summer solstice,
nces on the altar-stone at Stonehenge—

eam, expands, elongates, twists & 'attenuates
nto leafen gold
vering for the quince'.

rc & parabolic
ent-oblique—'musical in ocular
ny'. Expanding, elongating, twisting
nuating.

compassing eye.
n and out, round as a ball—
hither and thither, as straight as a line.
as a fox-whisker,
d, twined—rayed as chicory-flower.

n and out, round as a ball—
hither and thither, as straight as a line.
ily, germander
ops-in-wine. With sweet-briar and
re and strawberry wire
olumbine.

RONALD JOHNSON

from LOVE'S LABOUR'S LOST (Act 1, Sc. 1)

Light seeking light doth light of light beguile:
So, ere you find where light in darkness lies,
Your light grows dark by losing of your eyes.

WILLIAM SHAKESPEARE

DO NOT GO GENTLE INTO THAT GOOD NIGHT

Do not go gentle into that good night,
Old age should burn and rave at close of day;
Rage, rage against the dying of the light.

Though wise men at their end know dark is right,
Because their words had forked no lightning they
Do not go gentle into that good night.

Good men, the last wave by, crying how bright
Their frail deeds might have danced in a green bay,
Rage, rage against the dying of the light.

Wild men who caught and sang the sun in flight,
And learn, too late, they grieved it on its way,
Do not go gentle into that good night.

Grave men, near death, who see with blinding sight
Blind eyes could blaze like meteors and be gay,
Rage, rage against the dying of the light.

And you, my father, there on the sad height,
Curse, bless, me now with your fierce tears, I pray.
Do not go gentle into that good night.
Rage, rage against the dying of the light.

DYLAN THOMAS

#812

A Light exists in Spring
Not present on the Year
At any other period—
When March is scarcely here

A Color stands abroad
On Solitary Fields
That Science cannot overtake
But Human Nature feels.

It waits upon the Lawn,
It shows the furthest Tree
Upon the furthest Slope you know
It almost speaks to you.

Then as Horizons step
Or Noons report away
Without the Formula of sound
It passes and we stay—

A quality of loss
Affecting our Content
As Trade had suddenly encroached
Upon a Sacrament.

EMILY DICKINSON

from THE SONG OF SONGS

My beloved spake, and said unto me,
"Rise up, my love, my fair one, and come away.
For, lo, the winter is past,
The rain is over and gone;
The flowers appear on the earth;
The time of the singing of birds is come,
And the voice of the turtle is heard in our land;
The fig tree putteth forth her green figs,
And the vines with the tender grape give a good smell.
Arise, my love, my fair one, and come away."

BOOK OF SOLOMON 1: 10–13

IN THE BEGINNING

In the beginning was the three-pointed star,
One smile of light across the empty face;
One bough of bone across the rooting air,
The substance forked that marrowed the first sun;
And, burning ciphers on the round of space,
Heaven and hell mixed as they spun.

In the beginning was the pale signature,
Three-syllabled and starry as the smile;
And after came the imprints on the water,
Stamp of the minted face upon the moon;
The blood that touched the crosstree and the grail
Touched the first cloud and left a sign.

In the beginning was the mounting fire
That set alight the weathers from a spark,
A three-eyed, red-eyed spark, blunt as a flower;
Life rose and spouted from the rolling seas,
Burst in the roots, pumped from the earth and rock
The secret oils that drive the grass.

In the beginning was the word, the word
That from the solid bases of the light
Abstracted all the letters of the void;
And from the cloudy bases of the breath
The word flowed up, translating to the heart
First characters of birth and death.

In the beginning was the secret brain.
The brain was celled and soldered in the thought
Before the pitch was forking to a sun;
Before the veins were shaking in their sieve,
Blood shot and scattered to the winds of light
The ribbed original of love.

DYLAN THOMAS

from DARKNESS

   . . . and all hearts
Were chill'd into a selfish prayer for light.
And they did live by watch fires—and the thrones,
The palaces of crowned kings—the huts,
The habitations of all things which dwell,
Were burnt for beacons; cities were consumed,
And men were gather'd round their blazing homes
To look once more into each other's face.
Happy were those who dwelt within the eye
Of the volcanos, and their mountain-torch:
A fearful hope was all the world contain'd;
Forests were set on fire—but hour by hour
They fell and faded—and the crackling trunks
Extinguish'd with a crash—and all was black.

LORD BYRON

THE SKYSCRAPER LOVES NIGHT

One by one lights of a skyscraper fling their checkering cross work on the
    velvet gown of night.

I believe the skyscraper loves night as a woman and brings her playthings
    she asks for, brings her a velvet gown,
And loves the white of her shoulders hidden under the dark feel of it all.

The masonry of steel looks to the night for somebody it loves,
He is a little dizzy and almost dances . . . waiting . . . dark . . .

CARL SANDBURG

You are the light of the world. A city set on a hill cannot be hid. Nor do men light a lamp and put it under a bushel, but on a stand, and it gives light to all in the house. Let your light so shine before men, that they may see your good works and give glory to your Father who is in heaven.

MATTHEW 5:14–16

from LIGHT

Hail holy light, ofspring of Heav'n first-born,
Or of th' Eternal Coeternal beam
May I express thee unblam'd? since God is light,
And never but in unapproached light
Dwelt from Eternitie, dwelt then in thee,
Bright effluence of bright essence increate.
Or hear'st thou rather pure Ethereal stream,
Whose Fountain who shall tell?

JOHN MILTON

[22]

from THE REPUBLIC

But have you remarked that sight is by far the most costly and complex piece of workmanship which the artificer of the senses ever contrived?

No, I never have, he said.

Then reflect; has the ear or voice need of any third or additional nature in order that the one may be able to hear and the other to be heard?

Nothing of the sort.

No, indeed, I replied; and the same is true of most, if not all, the other senses—you would not say that any of them requires such an addition?

Certainly not.

But you see that without the addition of some other nature there is no seeing or being seen?

How do you mean?

Sight being, as I conceive, in the eyes, and he who has eyes wanting to see; colour being also present in them, still unless there be a third nature specially adapted to the purpose, the owner of the eyes will see nothing and the colours will be invisible.

Of what nature are you speaking?

Of that which you term light, I replied.

PLATO

FLUTE NOTES
FROM A REEDY POND

Now coldness comes sifting down, layer after layer,
To our bower at the lily root.
Overhead the old umbrellas of summer
Wither like pithless hands. There is little shelter.

Hourly the eye of the sky enlarges its blank
Dominion. The stars are no nearer.
Already frog-mouth and fish-mouth drink
The liquor of indolence, and all things sink

Into a soft caul of forgetfulness.
The fugitive colors die.
Caddis worms drowse in their silk cases,
The lamp-headed nymphs are nodding to sleep like statues.

Puppets, loosed from the strings of the puppet-master,
Wear masks of horn to bed.
This is not death, it is something safer.
The wingy myths won't tug at us any more:

The molts are tongueless that sang from above the water
Of golgotha at the tip of a reed,
And how a god flimsy as a baby's finger
Shall unhusk himself and steer into the air.

SYLVIA PLATH

ARIA

Music lifting and falling,
Waiting itself below,
The bowl at the base of the fountain
Spilling the overflow
In streams of silk and silver
To runnels underground.
The music is more like water
In pattern than in sound.
Moreover, hear this music
And see this water rise
In light almost more brilliant
Than that of Paradise,
Light beyond light, revealing
No fleck of time, no trace
Of cloud, no bar of shadow
To mark the dial's face.
The double rush and cadence
Of intricate delight,
Music lifting and falling,
Like water, pure and bright,
And light, beyond all radiance,
Intense, complete, profound,
No cloud on the golden mountain,
No shade on the golden ground.

ROLFE HUMPHRIES

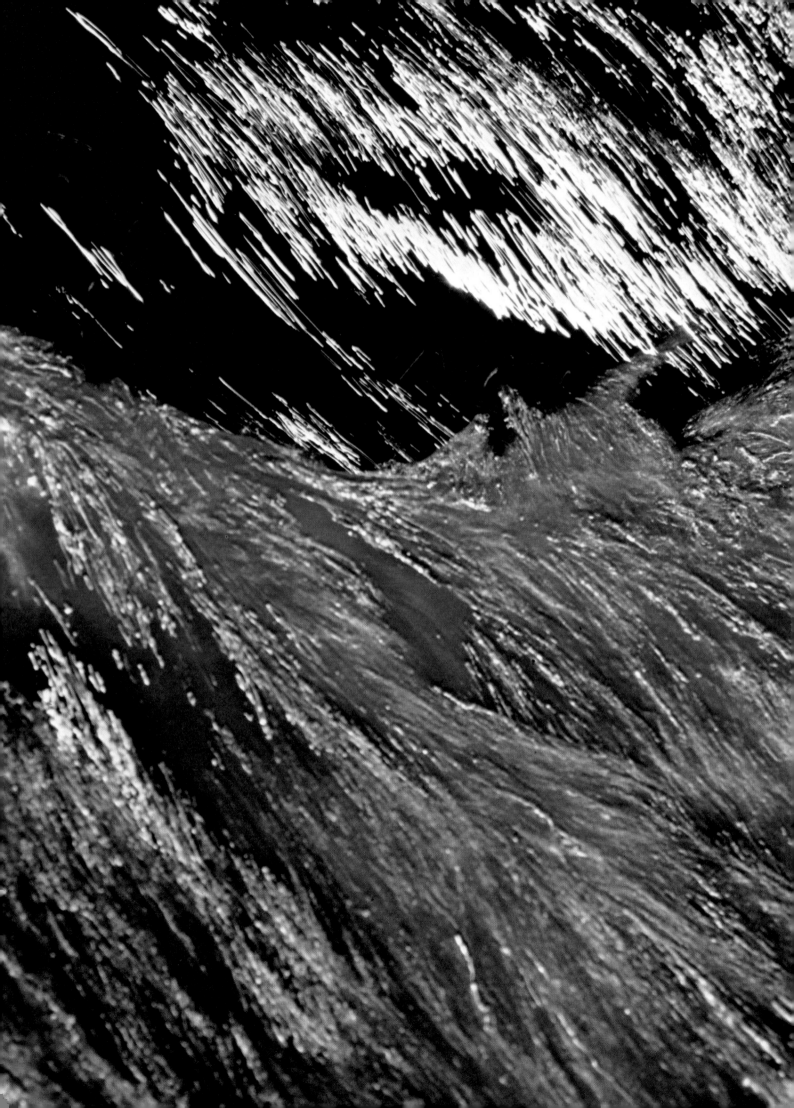

Daylight will peep through a very small hole.

JAPANESE PROVERB

THE RED BRANCH

Sky after sky of windless blue;
warm days, but with a secret chill.
The forest wall is green except
for one red branch on the hill.

Quiet the leaves, as on a board
dead butterflies are pinned,
except for one red branch that stirs
in premonition of a wind.

Soon the September gale, too soon
the bare branch, the leaves blown.
Now, in the mid-September truce,
    one leaf drifts down.

MALCOLM COWLEY

from THE TIME I'VE LOST

The light, that lies
In woman's eyes,
Has been my heart's undoing.

THOMAS MOORE

THE FLASH

Something far off   buried deep and free
In the country   can always strike you dead
Center of the brain. There is never anything

It could be   but you go dazzled
Dazzled   and all the air in that
Direction swarms   waits

For that day-lightning,
For hoe blade   buckle   bifocal
To reach you. Whatever it does

Again is worth waiting for
Worth stopping the car   worth standing alone
For   and arranging the body

For light to score off you
In its own way, and send
Across the wheat   the broad silent

Blue valley, your long-awaited,
Blinding, blood-brotherly
Beyond-speech answer.

JAMES DICKEY

from COMPOSITION IN GOLD AND RED-GOLD

Between the event and the word, golden
The sunlight falls, between
The brown brook's braiding and the mountain it
Falls, in pitiless plenitude, and every leaf
On the ruined apple tree is gold, and the apples all
Gold, too, especially those

On the ground. The gold of apples
That have fallen flushes to flame, but
Gold is the flame. Gold
Goes red-gold—and the scene:

A chipmunk is under the apple tree, sits up
Among gold apples, is
Golden in gold light. The chipmunk
Wriggles its small black nose
In the still center of the world of light.

The hair of the little girl is as brown-gold as
Brook water braiding in sunlight.

The cat, crouching by the gray stone, is gold, too.
The tail of the cat, half-Persian, weaves from side to side,
In infinite luxury, gold plume
Of sea-weed in that tide of light.
That is a motion that puts
The world to sleep.

ROBERT PENN WARREN

from WALDEN

The light which puts out our eyes is darkness to us. Only that day dawns
to which we are awake. There is more day to dawn. The sun is but a
morning star.

HENRY DAVID THOREAU

"The sun is new every day"

HERACLITUS

The morning has gold in its mouth.

DUTCH PROVERB

THE SUNNE RISING

     Busie old foole, unruly Sunne,
     Why dost thou thus,
Through windowes, and through curtaines call on us?
Must to thy motions lovers seasons run?
      Sawcy pedantique wretch, goe chide
      Late schoole boyes, and sowre prentices,
  Goe tell Court-huntsmen, that the King will ride,
  Call countrey ants to harvest offices;
Love, all alike, no season knowes, nor clyme,
Nor houres, dayes, moneths, which are the rags of time.

     Thy beames, so reverend, and strong
     Why shouldst thou thinke?
I could eclipse and cloud them with a winke,
But that I would not lose her sight so long:
      If her eyes have not blinded thine,
      Looke, and to morrow late, tell mee,
  Whether both the 'India's of spice and Myne
  Be where thou leftst them, or lie here with mee.
Aske for those Kings whom thou saw'st yesterday,
And thou shalt heare, All here in one bed lay.

     She'is all States, and all Princes, I,
     Nothing else is.
Princes doe but play us; compar'd to this,
All honor's mimique; All wealth alchimie;
      Thou sunne art halfe as happy'as wee,
      In that the world's contracted thus.
  Thine age askes ease, and since thy duties bee
  To warme the world, that's done in warming us.
Shine here to us, and thou art every where;
This bed thy center is, these walls, thy spheare.

JOHN DONNE

from DAY

The Sun arises in the East
Clothd in robes of blood & gold
Swords & spears & wrath increast
All around his bosom rolld
Crownd with warlike fires & raging desires

WILLIAM BLAKE

from the Introduction to PIPPA PASSES

Day!
Faster and more fast,
O'er night's brim, day boils at last;
Boils, pure gold, o'er the cloud cup's brim

ROBERT BROWNING

TATTOO

The light is like a spider.
It crawls over the water.
It crawls over the edges of the snow.
It crawls under your eyelids
And spreads its webs there—
Its two webs.

The webs of your eyes
Are fastened
To the flesh and bones of you
As to rafters or grass.

There are filaments of your eyes
On the surface of the water
And in the edges of the snow.

WALLACE STEVENS

SECURITY

There is refuge in a sea-shell—
Or a star;
But in between,
Nowhere.

There is peace in the immense—
Or the small;
Between the two,
Not at all.

The planet in the sky,
The sea-shell on the ground:
And though all heaven and earth
               between them lie,
No peace is to be found
Elsewhere.

Oh you who turn
For refuge, learn
From women, who have always known
The only roads that life has shown

To be secure.
How sure
The path a needle follows—or a star;
The near—the far.
With what compare
The light reflected from a thimble's stare,
Unless, on high,
Arcturus' eye?

The near—the far:
But in between,
Oh where
Is comfort to be seen?

There is refuge in a sea-shell—
Or a star;
But in between,
Nowhere.

ANNE MORROW LINDBERGH

A PRAIRIE SUNSET

Shot gold, maroon and violet, dazzling silver, emerald, fawn,
The earth's whole amplitude and Nature's multiform power consign'd
     for once to colors;
The light, the general air possess'd by them—colors till now unknown,
No limit, confine—not the Western sky alone—the high meridian—
     North, South, all,
Pure luminous color fighting the silent shadows to the last.

WALT WHITMAN

PIED BEAUTY

Glory be to God for dappled things—
    For skies of couple-colour as a brinded cow;
      For rose-moles all in stipple upon trout that swim;
Fresh-firecoal chestnut-falls; finches' wings;
    Landscape plotted and pieced—fold, fallow, and plough;
      And all trades, their gear and tackle and trim.
All things counter, original, spare, strange;
    Whatever is fickle, freckled (who knows how?)
      With swift, slow; sweet, sour; adazzle, dim;
He fathers-forth whose beauty is past change:
               Praise him.

                    GERARD MANLEY HOPKINS

from CHRISTABEL

A tongue of light, a fit of flame

SAMUEL TAYLOR COLERIDGE

from THE DIARY OF A YOUNG GIRL

No one had anything to suggest, so we simply sat there in pitch-darkness, because Mrs. Van Daan in her fright had unintentionally turned the lamp right out. . .

Footsteps in the house, in the private office, kitchen, then . . . on our staircase. No one breathed audibly now, footsteps on our staircase, then a rattling of the swinging cupboard. This moment is indescribable. ''Now we are lost!'' I said, and could see us all being taken away by the Gestapo that very night. Twice they rattled at the cupboard, then there was nothing, the footsteps withdrew, we were saved so far. A shiver seemed to pass from one to another. . . .

There was not another sound in the house, but a light was burning on our landing, right in front of the cupboard. Could that be because it was a secret cupboard? Perhaps the police had forgotten the light? Would someone come back to put it out?

ANNE FRANK

from A FEW FIGS FROM THISTLES

My candle burns at both ends;
    It will not last the night;
But ah, my foes, and oh, my friends—
    It gives a lovely light!

EDNA ST. VINCENT MILLAY

THE SECOND COMING

Turning and turning in the widening gyre
The falcon cannot hear the falconer;
Things fall apart; the centre cannot hold;
Mere anarchy is loosed upon the world,
The blood-dimmed tide is loosed, and everywhere
The ceremony of innocence is drowned;
The best lack all conviction, while the worst
Are full of passionate intensity.

Surely some revelation is at hand;
Surely the Second Coming is at hand.
The Second Coming! Hardly are those words out
When a vast image out of *Spiritus Mundi*
Troubles my sight: somewhere in sands of the desert
A shape with lion body and the head of a man
A gaze blank and pitiless as the sun,
Is moving its slow thighs, while all about is
Reel shadows of the indignant desert birds
The darkness drops again; but now I know
That twenty centuries of stony sleep
Were vexed to nightmare by a rocking cradle,
And what rough beast, its hour come round at last,
Slouches towards Bethlehem to be born?

WILLIAM BUTLER YEATS

from MOONLIGHT

As a pale phantom with a lamp
   Ascends some ruin's haunted stair,
So glides the moon along the damp
   Mysterious chambers of the air.

Now hidden in cloud, and now revealed,
   As if this phantom, full of pain,
Were by the crumbling walls concealed,
   And at the windows seen again.

Until at last, serene and proud
   In all the splendor of her light,
She walks the terraces of cloud,
   Supreme as Empress of the Night.

      HENRY WADSWORTH LONGFELLOW

THE STARLIGHT NIGHT

Look at the stars! look, look up at the skies!
O look at all the fire-folk sitting in the air!
The bright boroughs, the circle-citadels there!
Down in dim woods the diamond delves! the elves'-eyes!
The gray lawns cold where gold, where quickgold lies!
Wind-beat whitebeam! airy abeles set on a flare!
Flake-doves sent floating forth at a farmyard scare!
Ah, well! it is all a purchase, all is a prize.

Buy then! bid then!—What?—Prayer, patience, alms, vows.
Look, look a May-mess, like on orchard boughs!
Look! March-bloom, like on mealed-with-yellow sallows!
These are indeed the barn; withindoors house
The shocks. This piece-bright paling shuts the spouse
Christ home, Christ and his mother and all his hallows.

      GERARD MANLEY HOPKINS

from THE DIVINE COMEDY, "Paradiso," Canto XXXI

For the divine light pierceth with such power
   The world, in measure of its complement
   Of worth, that naught against it may endure.

      DANTE ALIGHIERI

from MODERN PAINTERS, "Of Turnerian Mystery"

Thus, when the eye is quite uncultivated, it sees that a man is a man, and a face is a face, but has no idea what shadows or lights fall upon the form or features. Cultivate it to some degree of artistic power, and it will then see shadows distinctly, but only the more vigorous of them. Cultivate it still farther, and it will see light within light, and shadow within shadow, and will continually refuse to rest in what it had already discovered, that it may pursue what is more removed and more subtle, until at last it comes to give its chief attention and display its chief power on gradations which to an untrained faculty are partly matters of indifference, and partly imperceptible.

JOHN RUSKIN

THE AGE OF SHEEN

I never see the colored boats of night
Jewelling the dull river, breaking their light
Upon it, without thinking of that age
Of sheen when the long poems are written,
The oblique books read until the exotic midges
Of the deep hours caper upon the page,
When there is time for the unlikely love,
And the mind, luxuriant in its sheath,
Wears the time shiningly, having no thought
Of the river, and the irony underneath.

DOROTHY HUGHES

NIGHT MOVEMENT—NEW YORK

In the night, when the sea-winds take the city in their arms,
And cool the loud streets that kept their dust noon and afternoon;
In the night, when the sea-birds call to the lights of the city,
The lights that cut on the skyline their name of a city;
In the night, when the trains and wagons start from a long way off
For the city where the people ask bread and want letters;
In the night the city lives too—the day is not all.
In the night there are dancers dancing and singers singing,
And the sailors and soldiers look for numbers on doors.
In the night the sea-winds take the city in their arms.

CARL SANDBURG

LIGHT

The night has a thousand eyes;
    And the day but one;
Yet the light of the bright world dies
    With the dying sun.

The mind has a thousand eyes,
    And the heart but one;
Yet the light of a whole life dies
    When love is done.

F. W. BOURDILLON

from PENSEES, Part 2

There is light enough for those who wish to see, and darkness enough for
those of the opposite disposition.

BLAISE PASCAL

POINT SHIRLEY

From Water-Tower Hill to the brick prison
The shingle booms, bickering under
The sea's collapse.
Snowcakes break and welter. This year
The gritted wave leaps
The seawall and drops onto a bier
Of quahog chips,
Leaving a salty mash of ice to whiten

In my grandmother's sand yard. She is dead,
Whose laundry snapped and froze here, who
Kept house against
What the sluttish, rutted sea could do.
Squall waves once danced
Ship timbers in through the cellar window;
A thresh-tailed, lanced
Shark littered in the geranium bed—

Such collusion of mulish elements
She wore her broom straws to the nub.
Twenty years out
Of her hand, the house still hugs in each drab
Stucco socket
The purple egg-stones: from Great Head's knob
To the filled-in Gut
The sea in its cold gizzard ground those rounds.

Nobody wintering now behind
The planked-up windows where she set
Her wheat loaves
And apple cakes to cool. What is it
Survives, grieves
So, over this battered, obstinate spit
Of gravel? The waves'
Spewed relics clicker masses in the wind,

Grey waves the stub-necked eiders ride.
A labor of love, and that labor lost.
Steadily the sea
Eats at Point Shirley. She died blessed,
And I come by
Bones, bones only, pawed and tossed,
A dog-faced sea.
The sun sinks under Boston, bloody red.

I would get from these dry-papped stones
The milk your love instilled in them.
The black ducks dive.
And though your graciousness might stream,
And I contrive,
Grandmother, stones are nothing of home
To that spumiest dove.
Against both bar and tower the black sea runs.

SYLVIA PLATH

from DOVER BEACH

The sea is calm to-night.
The tide is full, the moon lies fair
Upon the straits;—on the French coast the light
Gleams and is gone; the cliffs of England stand,
Glimmering and vast, out in the tranquil bay.
Come to the window, sweet is the night-air!

Only, from the long line of spray
Where the sea meets the moon-blanch'd land,
Listen! you hear the grating roar
Of pebbles which the waves draw back, and fling,
At their return, up the high strand,
Begin, and cease, and then again begin,
With tremulous cadence slow, and bring
The eternal note of sadness in.

MATTHEW ARNOLD

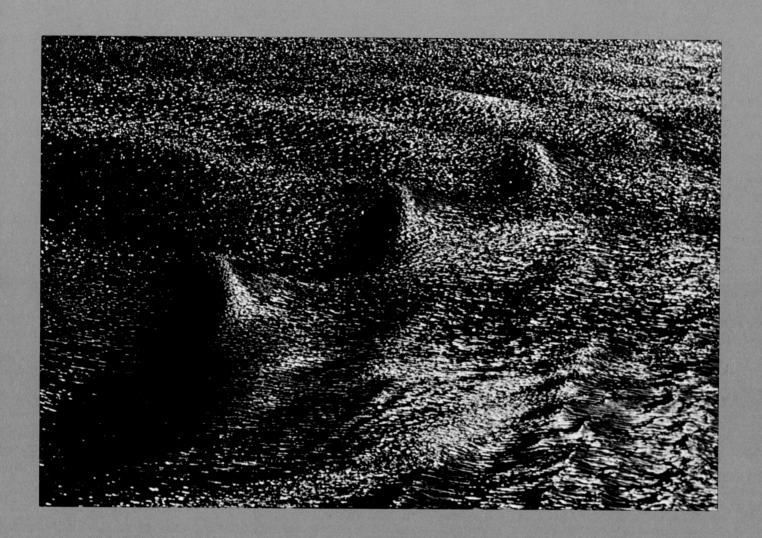

from THE REPUBLIC,
"The Parable of the Lights in the Cave"

And now, I said, let me show in a figure how far our nature is enlightened or unenlightened:—Behold! human beings living in an underground den, which has a mouth open towards the light and reaching all along the den; here they have been from their childhood, and have their legs and necks chained so that they cannot move, and can only see before them, being prevented by the chains from turning round their heads. Above and behind them a fire is blazing at a distance, and between the fire and the prisoners there is a raised way; and you will see, if you look, a low wall built along the way, like the screen which marionette players have in front of them, over which they show the puppets.

I see.

And do you see, I said, men passing along the wall carrying all sorts of vessels, and statues and figures of animals made of wood and stone and various materials, which appear over the wall? Some of them are talking, others silent.

You have shown me a strange image, and they are strange prisoners.

Like ourselves, I replied; and they see only their own shadows, or the shadows of one another, which the fire throws on the opposite wall of the cave?

True, he said; how could they see anything but the shadows if they were never allowed to move their heads?

And of the objects which are being carried in like manner they would only see the shadows?

Yes, he said.

And if they were able to converse with one another, would they not suppose that they were naming what was actually before them?

Very true.

And suppose further that the prison had an echo which came from the other side, would they not be sure to fancy when one of the passers-by spoke that the voice which they heard came from the passing shadow?

No question, he replied.

To them, I said, the truth would be literally nothing but the shadows of the images.

That is certain.

And now look again, and see what will naturally follow if the prisoners are released and disabused of their error. At first, when any of them is liberated and compelled suddenly to stand up and turn his neck round and walk and look towards the light, he will suffer sharp pains; the glare will distress him, and he will be unable to see the realities of which in his former state he had seen the shadows; and then conceive some one saying to him, that what he saw before was an illusion, but that now, when he is approaching nearer to being and his eye is turned towards more real existence, he has a clearer vision,—what will be his reply? And you may further imagine that his instructor is pointing to the objects as they pass and requiring him to name them,—will he not be perplexed? Will he not fancy that the shadows which he formerly saw are truer than the objects which are now shown to him?

Far truer.

And if he is compelled to look straight at the light, will he not have a pain in his eyes which will make him turn away to take refuge in the objects of vision which he can see, and which he will conceive to be in reality clearer than the things which are now being shown to him?

True, he said.

And suppose once more, that he is reluctantly dragged up a steep and rugged ascent, and held fast until he is forced into the presence of the sun himself, is he not likely to be pained and irritated? When he approaches the light his eyes will be dazzled, and he will not be able to see anything at all of what are now called realities.

Not all in a moment, he said.

He will require to grow accustomed to the sight of the upper world. And first he will see the shadows best, next the reflections of men and other objects in the water, and then the objects themselves; then he will gaze upon the light of the moon and the stars and the spangled heaven; and he will see the sky and the stars by night better than the sun or the light of the sun by day?

Certainly.

Last of all he will be able to see the sun, and not mere reflections of him in the water, but he will see him in his own proper place, and not in another; and he will contemplate him as he is.

Certainly.

He will then proceed to argue that this is he who gives the season and the years, and is the guardian of all that is in the visible world, and in a certain way the cause of all things which he and his fellows have been accustomed to behold?

Clearly, he said, he would first see the sun and then reason about him.

And when he remembered his old habitation, and the wisdom of the den and his fellow-prisoners, do you not suppose that he would felicitate himself on the change, and pity them?

Certainly, he would.

And if they were in the habit of conferring honours among themselves on those who were quickest to observe the passing shadows and to remark which of them went before, and which followed after, and which were together; and who were therefore best able to draw conclusions as to the future, do you think that he would care for such honours and glories, or envy the possessors of them? Would he not say with Homer,

'Better to be the poor servant of a poor master,'

and to endure anything, rather than think as they do and live after their manner?

Yes, he said, I think that he would rather suffer anything than entertain these false notions and live in this miserable manner.

Imagine once more, I said, such an one coming suddenly out of the sun to be replaced in his old situation; would he not be certain to have his eyes full of darkness?

To be sure, he said.

And if there were a contest, and he had to compete in measuring the shadows with the prisoners who had never moved out of the den, while his sight was still weak, and before his eyes had become steady (and the time which would be needed to acquire this new habit of sight might be very considerable) would he not be ridiculous? Men would say of him that up he went and down he came without his eyes; and that it was better not even to think of ascending; and if any one tried to loose another and lead him up to the light, let them only catch the offender, and they would put him to death.

No question, he said.

This entire allegory, I said, you may now append, dear Glaucon, to the previous argument; the prisonhouse is the world of sight, the light of the fire is the sun, and you will not misapprehend me if you interpret the journey upwards to be the ascent of the soul into the intellectual world according to my poor belief, which, at your desire, I have expressed—whether rightly or wrongly God knows. But, whether true or false, my opinion is that in the world of knowledge the idea of good appears last of all, and is seen only with an effort; and, when seen, is also inferred to be the universal author of all things beautiful and right, parent of light and of the lord of light in this visible world, and the immediate source of reason and truth in the intellectual; and that this is the power upon which he who would act rationally either in public or private life must have his eye fixed.

PLATO

from THE RAINBOW

                                    See on one hand
He drops his bright roots in the water'd sward,
And rosing part, on part dispenses green;
But with his other foot three miles beyond
He rises from the flocks of villages
That bead the plain; did ever Havering church-tower
Breathe in such ether? . . . or the Quickly elms
Slight with such violet their bright-mask'd green?

GERARD MANLEY HOPKINS

AUGUST RAINBOWS

And after every summer rain
an August rainbow
sunlight in the good green wood
laughter in the town
shelter in the noontime shadows
or here inside each other's arms.

No one can kill our rainbows
though sometimes the world
seems bent on trying.

ROD McKUEN

light, *n*. 1. that which makes things visible or affords illumination: *All colors depend on light*.

THE RANDOM HOUSE DICTIONARY OF THE ENGLISH LANGUAGE

THE USES OF LIGHT

It warms my bones
          say the stones

I take it into me and grow
Say the trees
Leaves above
Roots below

A vast vague white
Draws me out of the night
Says the moth in his flight—

Some things I smell
Some things I hear
And I see things move
Says the deer—

A high tower
on a wide plain.
If you climb up
One floor
You'll see a thousand miles more.

GARY SNYDER

FIRE AND ICE

Some say the world will end in fire,
Some say in ice.
From what I've tasted of desire
I hold with those who favor fire.
But if it had to perish twice,
I think I know enough of hate
To say that for destruction ice
Is also great
And would suffice.

ROBERT FROST

[66]

from AUTUMN SHADE

Not shadows but substantial light, explicit,
Bright as glass, inexhaustible, and true.

EDGAR BOWERS

Where there is much light, the shade is deepest.

GOETHE

Any patch of sunlight in a wood will show you something about the sun which you could never get from reading books on astronomy. These pure and spontaneous pleasures are patches of Godlight in the woods of our experience.

C. S. LEWIS

from TO MARK ANTHONY IN HEAVEN

This quiet morning light
reflected, how many times
from grass and trees and clouds
enters my north room
touching the walls with
grass and clouds and trees.

WILLIAM CARLOS WILLIAMS

SONNET 65

Since brass, nor stone, nor earth, nor boundless sea,
But sad mortality o'ersways their power,
How with this rage shall beauty hold a plea,
Whose action is no stronger than a flower?
O how shall summer's honey breath hold out
Against the wrackful siege of batt'ring days,
When rocks impregnable are not so stout,
Nor gates of steel so strong but time decays?
O fearful meditation, where alack,
Shall time's best jewel from time's chest lie hid?
Or what strong hand can hold his swift foot back,
Or how his spoil of beauty can forbid?
    O none, unless this miracle have might,
    That in black ink my love may still shine bright.

WILLIAM SHAKESPEARE

from THE LITTLE PRINCE

The little prince was now white with rage.

"The flowers have been growing thorns for millions of years. For millions of years the sheep have been eating them just the same. And is it not a matter of consequence to try to understand why the flowers go to so much trouble to grow thorns which are never of any use to them? Is the warfare between the sheep and the flowers not important? Is this not of more consequence than a fat red-faced gentleman's sums? And if I know—I, myself—one flower which is unique in the world, which grows nowhere but on my planet, but which one little sheep can destroy in a single bite some morning, without even noticing what he is doing—Oh! You think that is not important!"

His face turned from white to red as he continued:

"If some one loves a flower, of which just one single blossom grows in all the millions and millions of stars, it is enough to make him happy just to look at the stars. He can say to himself: "Somewhere, my flower is there . . .' But if the sheep eats the flower, in one moment all his stars will be darkened . . . And you think that is not important!"

He could not say anything more. His words were choked by sobbing. . . .

I did not know what to say to him. . . .

It is such a secret place, the land of tears.

ANTOINE DE SAINT-EXUPERY

DAWN

Suddenly. Is. Now not what was *not*,
But what is. From nothing of *not*
Now all of *is*. All is. Is light, and suddenly
Dawn—and the world in blaze of *is*,
Burns. Is flame, of time and tense
The bold combustion, and
The flame of *is*, in fury
And ungainsayable updraft of that
Black chimney of what is *not*,
Roars. Christmas—

Remember, remember!—and into flame
All those gay wrappings the children fling, then
In hands of *now*, they hold
Presents of *is*, and while
Flame leaps, they in joy,
Scream. Oh, children,

Now to me sing, I see
Forever on the leaf the light. Snow
On the pine-leaf, against the bright blue
Forever of my mind, like breath,
Balances, but light,

Is always light, and suddenly,
On any morning, is, and somewhere,
In a garden you will never
See, dew, in fracture of light
And lunacy of gleam-glory, glitters on
A petal red as blood, and

The rose dies, laughing.

ROBERT PENN WARREN

TRANSCONTINENTAL, 1910

When I was young of limb and brain
My mother took me West by train.
It seemed the natural thing to do;
We couldn't drive, and no one flew.

We might have gone some other way,
But Father chose the Santa Fe;
And that was good enough for me
(The ballad called it "Santa Fee").

I still remember how the plains
Slid past the double windowpanes
Till evening with its pinky tinge
Put mountains on the desert fringe,

And then I'm lonely in my bed.
The engine whistles far ahead,
And far away one prairie light
Shines fainter than the stars that night.

Or I can wake one morning young
In country of the cactus-tongue,
And eat my breakfast dreaming back
Along the spirals of the track.

I doubt if Harvey knew his name
Could burn as did his charcoal flame,
But have potatoes touched again
The skins he baked in nineteen-ten?

Don't tell me now his bill of fare
Includes both venison and *bear*—
That word, as magical as fate,
Is black meat on a magic plate.

Then somewhere, after endless miles
Of endless view or dark defiles,
I'm seated on a squeaky stool,
Out of the night wind blowing cool,

Tasting a queer concocted dish—
"You'll like it, son!" I made a wish,
But what it was is lost in rings
Of lantern light and broken springs

And shouting men, and round a truck
The wrecking crew—abiding luck.
We walked the platform east and west:
One way was home and one the quest,

And one was sad with late goodbyes,
And one Sierras and surprise,
And one was grief and all but gone.
And one was rising in the dawn. . . .

A river ran next morning white
With pelicans in foreign flight,
And something of a boy I'd lost
Knew then how great a range was crossed.

DAVID MCCORD

ON A DROP OF DEW

See how the Orient Dew,
Shed from the Bosom of the Morn
    Into the blowing Roses,
Yet careless of its Mansion new;
For the clear Region where 'twas born
    Round in its self incloses:
    And in its little Globes Extent,
Frames as it can its native Element.
    How it the purple flow'r does slight,
        Scarce touching where it lyes,
    But gazing back upon the Skies,
        Shines with a mournful Light;
        Like its own Tear,
Because so long divided from the Sphear.
    Restless it roules and unsecure,
        Trembling lest it grow impure:
    Till the warm Sun pitty it's Pain,
And to the Skies exhale it back again.
        So the Soul, that Drop, that Ray
Of the clear Fountain of Eternal Day,
Could it within the humane flow'r be seen,
        Remembring still its former height,
        Shuns the sweat leaves and blossoms green;
        And, recollecting its own Light,
Does, in its pure and circling thoughts, express
The greater Heaven in an Heaven less.
        In how coy a Figure wound,
        Every way it turns away:
        So the World excluding round,
        Yet receiving in the Day.
        Dark beneath, but bright above:
        Here disdaining, there in Love.
    How loose and easie hence to go:
    How girt and ready to ascend.
    Moving but on a point below,
    It all about does upwards bend.
Such did the Manna's sacred Dew destil;
White, and intire, though congeal'd and chill.
Congeal'd on Earth : but does, dissolving, run
Into the Glories of th' Almighty Sun.

ANDREW MARVELL

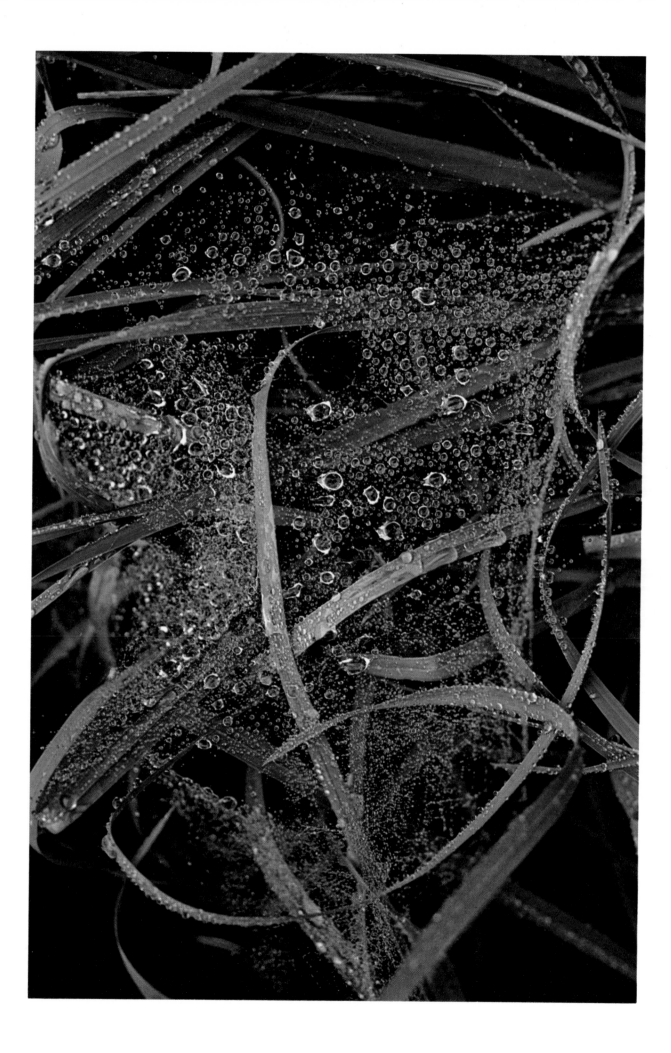

SCHATTEN KUESSE, SCHATTEN LIEBE

after Heine

Shadow kisses, shadow love,
There is nothing else left now—
Faint electric traces
In the nerve cells of two brains.

The rain falls in the deep night—
Black streets, a distant city—
Far away, too far away—
Yes? Too far away from where?

Too far from time which passes?
Too far from flesh breaking change?
Too far from happiness
Which would not wait an instant?

Two heads alone in dark rooms,
Far apart in rainy night,
Shelter sparks of memory,
Lamps once blazing with kisses.

KENNETH REXROTH

PATTERN

Some believe the slumber
Of trees is in December
   When timber's naked under sky
And squirrel keeps his chamber.

But I believe their fibres
Awake to life and labour
   When turbulence comes roaring up
The land in loud October,

And plunders, strips, and sunders
And sends the leaves to wander
   And undisguises prickly shapes
Beneath the golden splendour.

Then form returns. In warmer,
Seductive days, disarming
   Its firmer will, the wood grew soft
And put forth dreams to murmur.

Into earnest winter
With spirit alert it enters;
   The hunter wind and the hound frost
Have quelled the green enchanter.

C. S. LEWIS

THIS AMBER SUNSTREAM

This amber sunstream, with an hour to live,
Flows carelessly, and does not save itself;
Nor recognizes any entered room—
This room; nor hears the clock upon a shelf,
Declaring the lone hour; for where it goes
All space in a great silence ever flows.

No living man may know it till this hour,
When the clear sunstream, thickening to amber,
Moves like a sea, and the sunk hulls of houses
Let it come slowly through, as divers clamber,
Feeling for gold. So now into this room
Peer the large eyes, unopen to their doom.

Another hour and nothing will be here.
Even upon themselves the eyes will close.
Nor will this bulk, withdrawing, die outdoors
In night, that from another silence flows.
No living man in any western room
But sits at amber sunset round a tomb.

MARK VAN DOREN

HE WISHES FOR THE CLOTHS OF HEAVEN

Had I the heavens' embroidered cloths,
Enwrought with golden and silver light,
The blue and the dim and the dark cloths
Of night and light and the half-light,
I would spread the cloths under your feet:
But I, being poor, have only my dreams;
I have spread my dreams under your feet;
Tread softly because you tread on my dreams.

WILLIAM BUTLER YEATS

from STUART LITTLE

"How many of you know what's important?"
Up went all the hands.
"Very good," said Stuart, cocking one leg across the other and shoving his hands in the pockets of his jacket. "Henry Rackmeyer, you tell us what is important."
"A shaft of sunlight at the end of a dark afternoon, a note in music, and the way the back of a baby's neck smells if its mother keeps it tidy," answered Henry.
"Correct," said Stuart. "Those are the important things. . ."

E. B. WHITE

CLOUDS

Over the coastal ranges slight and indefinite clouds
Moved in to sunrise, rode up the west;
Toward noon the change of the wind strung them to furrows.
Sundown flared late, the close and the heavy twilight of August hooded
    the fields.
They were broken to fragments, and were burnt on the growth of the
    gathering night,
When Venus blazed west and went down.

So common a beauty: the workers over the wide fields hardly looked up.
Under the great arching sky of the valley the clouds are across us,
The trade of the routes of the upper air,
Their temporal splendor hawked on the wind for some listless eye.

Cirrus and stratus: the fringe of the distant storms of the sea;
December wanes and the numbus are driving.
They are scattered by dawns, or are killed on the heavy fists of the peaks;
But the wind breeds them west forever.

[86]

WILLIAM EVERSON

from THE LEAF

In the momentary silence of the cicada,
I can hear the appalling speed,
In space beyond stars, of
Light. It is

A sound like wind.

ROBERT PENN WARREN

from PRELUDE

For instantly a light upon the turf
Fell like a flash, and lo! as I looked up,
The Moon hung naked in a firmament
Of azure without cloud, and at my feet
Rested a silent sea of hoary mist.

WILLIAM B. WORDSWORTH

from "I STOOD TIP-TOE UPON A LITTLE HILL"

Or by the moon lifting her silver rim
Above a cloud, and with a gradual swim
Coming into the blue with all her light.
O Maker of sweet poets, dear delight
Of this fair world, and all its gentle livers;
Spangler of clouds, halo of crystal rivers,
Mingler with leaves, and dew and tumbling streams,
Closer of lovely eyes to lovely dreams,
Lover of loneliness, and wandering,
Of upcast eye, and tender pondering!
Thee must I praise above all other glories
That smile us on to tell delightful stories.
For what has made the sage or poet write
But the fair paradise of Nature's light?

JOHN KEATS

from NIGHT

The moon like a flower
In heaven's high bower,
With silent delight
Sits and smiles on the night.

WILLIAM BLAKE

SUNDOWN

The summer sun is sinking low;
Only the tree-tops redden and glow;
Only the weathercock on the spire
Of the neighboring church is a flame of fire
    All is in shadow below.

O beautiful, awful summer day,
What hast thou given, what taken away?
Life and death, and love and hate,
Homes made happy or desolate,
    Hearts made sad or gay!

On the road of life one mile-stone more!
In the book of life one leaf turned o'er!
Like a red seal is the setting sun
On the good and the evil men have done,—
    Naught can to-day restore!

HENRY WADSWORTH LONGFELLOW

AFTERGLOW

Sunset is always disturbing
whether theatrical or muted,
but still more disturbing
is that last desperate glow
that turns the plain to rust
when on the horizon nothing is left
of the pomp and clamor of the setting sun.
How hard holding on to that light, so tautly drawn and different,
that hallucination which the human fear of the dark
imposes on space
and which ceases at once
the moment we realize its falsity,
the way a dream is broken
the moment the sleeper knows he is dreaming.

JORGE LUIS BORGES

(Translated from the Spanish by Norman Thomas di Giovanni)

from MEMORIES, DREAMS, REFLECTIONS

As far as we can discern, the sole purpose of human existence is to kindle
a light in the darkness of mere being.

CARL JUNG

The first creature of God, in the works of the days, was the light of sense:
the last was the light of reason: and his sabbath work ever since is the
illumination of his Spirit.

FRANCIS BACON

LITTLE CANDLE

Light may be had for nothing
or the low cost of looking, seeing;
and the secrets of light come high.
Light knows more than it tells.
Does it happen the sun, the moon
choose to be dazzling, baffling?
They do demand deep loyal communions.
So do the angles of moving stars.
So do the seven sprays of the rainbow.
So does any little candle
speaking for itself in its personal corner.

CARL SANDBURG

THE BLIND MEN AND THE ELEPHANT
(A Hindoo Fable)

It was six men of Indostan
   To learning much inclined,
Who went to see the Elephant
   (Though all of them were blind),
That each by observation
   Might satisfy his mind.

The *First* approached the Elephant,
   And happening to fall
Against his broad and sturdy side,
   At once began to bawl:
"God bless me! but the Elephant
   Is very like a wall!"

The *Second*, feeling of the tusk,
   Cried, "Ho! what have we here
So very round and smooth and sharp?
   To me 'tis mighty clear
This wonder of an Elephant
   Is very like a spear!"

The *Third* approached the animal,
   And happening to take
The squirming trunk within his hands,
   Thus boldly up and spake:
"I see," quoth he, "the Elephant
   Is very like a snake!"

The *Fourth* reached out an eager hand,
   And felt about the knee.
"What most this wondrous beast is like
   Is mighty plain," quoth he;
"'Tis clear enough the Elephant
   Is very like a tree!"

The *Fifth* who chanced to touch the ear,
   Said: "E'en the blindest man
Can tell what this resembles most;
   Deny the fact who can,
This marvel of an Elephant
   Is very like a fan!"

The *Sixth* no sooner had begun
   About the beast to grope,
Than, seizing on the swinging tail
   That fell within his scope,
"I see," quoth he, "the Elephant
   Is very like a rope!"

And so these men of Indostan
   Disputed loud and long,
Each in his own opinion
   Exceeding stiff and strong,
Though each was partly in the right,
   And all were in the wrong!

Moral
So oft in theologic wars,
   The disputants, I ween,
Rail on in utter ignorance
   Of what the others mean,
And prate about an Elephant
   Not one of them has seen!

JOHN GODFREY SAXE

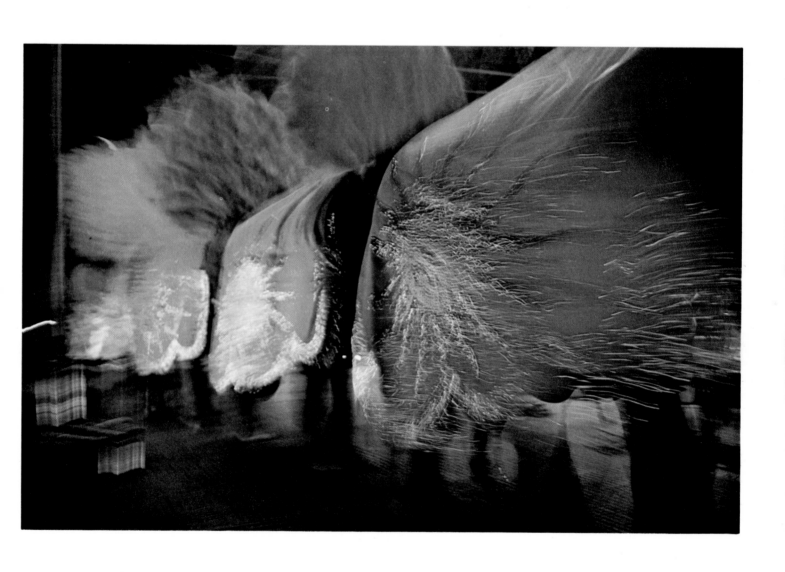

I

Just so it goes—the day, the night,
what have you. There is no one on TV.
Shadows in the tube, in the street.
In the telephone, there are echoes and mumblings,
the buzz of hours falling through wires.

And hollow socks stumbling across
the ceiling send plaster dust sifting down
hourglass walls. Felix the cat has
been drawn on retinas with a pencil of light.
I wait, gray, small in my cranny,

for the cardboard tiger on the
kitchen table to snap me, shredded, from
the bowl.

II

Over the trestle go
the steel beetles, grappled tooth-to-tail—over and
over and over, there, smokestacks

lung tall hawkers into the sky's
spittoon. The street has a black tongue. Do you
hear him, Mistress Alley, wooing
you with stones? There are phantoms in that roof's
trousers;
they kick the wind. The moon, on a

ladder, is directing traffic
now. You can hardly hear his whistle. The
oculist's jeep wears horn-rimmed wind-
shields, the motor wears wires on its overhead valves.
Grow weary, weary, sad siren,

you old whore. It's time to retire.

III

The wail of the child in the next room quails
like a silverfish caught in a
thread. It is quiet now. The child's sigh rises to
flap with a cormorant's grace through

the limbo of one lamp and a
slide-viewer in your fingers. I cannot
get thin enough for light to shine
my color in your eyes. There is no frame but this for
the gathering of the clan. Words

will stale the air. Come, gather up
our voices in the silent butler and
pour them into the ashcan of
love. Look, my nostrils are dual flues; my ears are
the city dump; my eyes are the

very soul of trash; my bitter
tongue tastes like gasoline in a littered
alley.

IV

The child cries again. Sounds
rise by the riverflats like smoke or mist in time's
bayou. We are sewn within seines

of our own being, thrown into
menaces floating in shadows, taken
without volition like silver
fish in an undertow down the river, down time,
and smogs of evening.

V

The child cries.

VI

Do you hear the voice made of wire?
Do you hear the child swallowed by carpets,
the alley eating the city,
rustling newsprint, in the street, begging moonlight with
a tin cup and a blindman's cane?

VII

The lamps are rheumy in these tar
avenues. Can you sense the droppings of
flesh falling between walls falling,
the burrowing of nerves in a cupboard of cans?
Can you hear the roar of the mouse?

VIII

There is nothing but the doorway
sighing; here there is nothing but the wind
swinging on its hinges, a fly
dusty with silence, and the house, on its back, buzzing
with chimneys, walking on the sky

like a blind man eating fish in an empty room.

LEWIS TURCO

THE BUCK IN THE SNOW

White sky, over the hemlocks bowed with snow,
Saw you not at the beginning of evening the antlered buck and his doe
Standing in the apple-orchard? I saw them. I saw them suddenly go,
Tails up, with long leaps lovely and slow,
Over the stone-wall into the wood of hemlocks bowed with snow.

Now lies he here, his wild blood scalding the snow.

How strange a thing is death, bringing to his knees, bringing to his
    antlers
The buck in the snow.
How strange a thing,—a mile away by now, it may be,
Under the heavy hemlocks that as the moments pass
Shift their loads a little, letting fall a feather of snow—
Life, looking out attentive from the eyes of the doe.

EDNA ST. VINCENT MILLAY

from WINTER DAY

The sun that brief December day
Rose cheerless over hills of gray,
And, darkly circled, gave at noon
A sadder light than waning moon.
Slow tracing down the thickening sky
Its mute and ominous prophecy,
A portent seeming less than threat,
It sank from sight before it set.
A chill no coat, however stout,
Of homespun stuff could quite shut out,
A hard, dull bitterness of cold,
That checked, mid-vein, the circling race
Of life-blood in the sharpened face
The coming of the snow-storm told.

JOHN GREENLEAF WHITTIER

BLUE FLAG

Blue as the blowpipe's petal of flame,
the flag, afloat at the crest of the wave
of its leaves, unfurls an ephemeral crown,
three-tiered, nine-rayed, and girdled with jade.

Sealed, to begin with, in tissue, and stuck
to the stem in a curve like a locust's wing,
it rides into light in this envelope lean
as a leaf, too thin to hold a thing,

it would seem, till it opens and shows a ship-
in-a-bottle surprise: slim as a moth
at birth stands an elegant spindle, sea purple
and patched with gold, that turns, no sloth

so slow, to a lily of chiselled gauze.
In curves as sharp as if carved with scalpels
from paper-thin slices of stone inked in,
pen-fine, with damson lines like the marble's

veins, it spreads its spurs. It shows
its colors in yellow carpets plumed
with plush for the feet of the bee as she feels
her way over azure bridges and perfumed

paths, through tunnels down to the well-hid
wells where the diamond drop of nectar
is. All this to bring, spring
after spring, the seed to the bud to the flower

to the bee, again, again, and again
with undiminished *esprit*, to bear,
once more, the same lambent form as before,
jewel-winged, a weld of blue fire and air.

DOROTHY DONNELLY

from WALDEN

The surface of the earth is soft and impressible by the feet of men; and so with the paths which the mind travels. How worn and dusty, then, must be the highways of the world, how deep the ruts of tradition and conformity! I did not wish to take a cabin passage, but rather to go before the mast and on the deck of the world, for there I can best see the moonlight amid the mountains. I do not wish to go below now.

HENRY DAVID THOREAU

A SUNSET

Upon the mountain's edge with light touch resting,
There a brief while the globe of splendour sits
    And seems a creature of the earth; but soon
        More changeful than the Moon,
To wane fantastic his great orb submits,
Or cone or mow of fire: till sinking slowly
Even to a star at length he lessens wholly.

Abrupt, as Spirits vanish, he is sunk!
A soul-like breeze possesses all the wood.
    The boughs, the sprays have stood
As motionless as stands the ancient trunk!
But every leaf through all the forest flutters,
And deep the cavern of the fountain mutters.

SAMUEL TAYLOR COLERIDGE

from LIGHT OF THE MOON

Mournful and lovely is the moon's calm light,
Which moves the bird upon the bough to dream
And makes the fountains sob in quick delight,
The slim tall fountains where the marbles gleam.

PAUL VERLAINE

"ASK ME NO MORE"

Ask me no more: the moon may draw the sea;
   The cloud may stoop from heaven and take the shape
   With fold to fold, of mountain or of cape;
But I too fond, when have I answer'd thee?
          Ask me no more.

Ask me no more: what answer should I give?
   I love not hollow cheek or faded eye:
   Yet, O my friend, I will not have thee die!
Ask me no more, lest I should bid thee live;
          Ask me no more.

Ask me no more: thy fate and mine are seal'd:
   I strove against the stream and all in vain:
   Let the great river take me to the main:
No more, dear love, for at a touch I yield;
          Ask me no more.

ALFRED, LORD TENNYSON

from MODERN PAINTERS, *"Of Typical Beauty"*

. . . the ocular delight in purity is mingled, as I before observed, with the love of the mere element of light, as a type of wisdom and of truth . . . whence it seems to me that we admire the transparency of bodies, though probably it is still rather owing to our sense of more perfect order and arrangement of particles, and not to our love of light, that we look upon a piece of rock crystal as purer than a piece of marble, and on the marble as purer than a piece of chalk. And let it be observed also that the most lovely objects in nature are only partially transparent. I suppose the utmost possible sense of beauty is conveyed by a feebly translucent, smooth, but not lustrous surface of white, and pale warm red, subdued by the most pure and delicate grays, as in the finer portions of the human frame; in wreaths of snow, and in white plumage under rose light, so Viola of Olivia in Twelfth Night, and Homer of Atrides wounded. And I think that transparency and lustre, both beautiful in themselves, are incompatible with the highest beauty because they destroy form, on the full perception of which more of the divinely character of the object depends than upon its color. Hence, in the beauty of snow and of flesh, so much translucency is allowed as is consistent with the full explanation of the forms, while we are suffered to receive more intense impressions of light and transparency from other objects which, nevertheless, owing to their necessarily unperceived form, are not perfectly nor affectingly beautiful. A fair forehead outshines its diamond diadem. The sparkle of the cascade withdraws not our eyes from the snowy summits in their evening silence.

JOHN RUSKIN

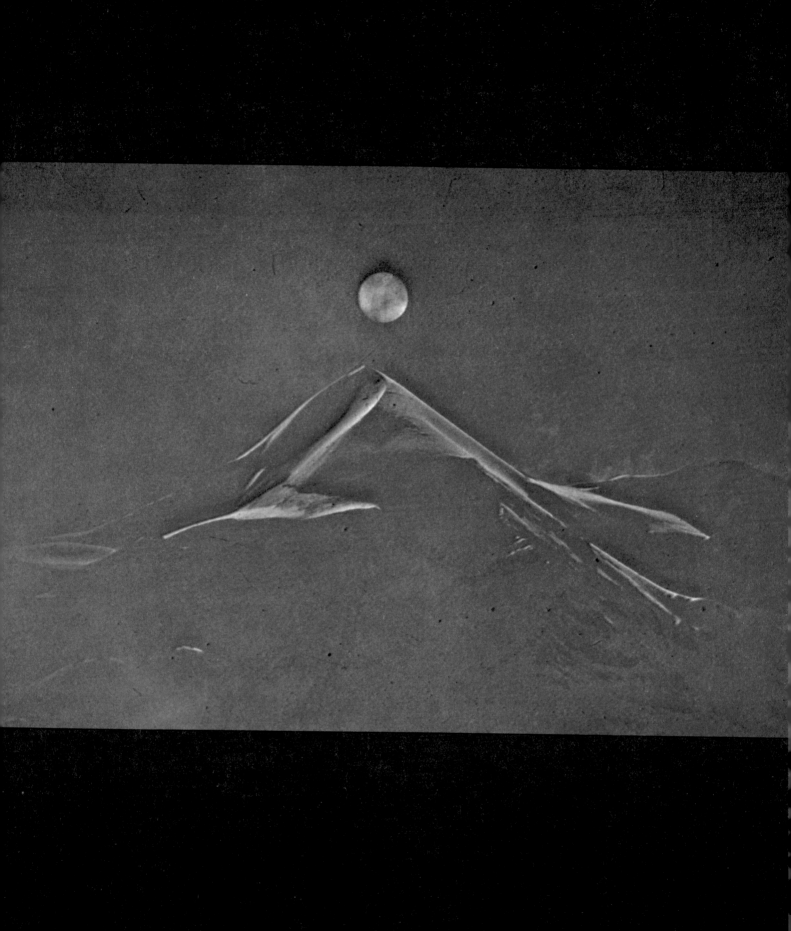

ERNST HAAS—GENERAL NOTES

I have always used Kodachrome film as it retains its color value for years; Kodachrome 25 has a fine definition and lack of grain. I almost never use a tripod, and I keep my equipment to a minimum because I prefer to travel light. I like to work with Leica M3 and M4 cameras, occasionally with Pentax cameras with Leica lenses attached. Since 1969 I also use the Leicaflex cameras and lenses. I work mainly with lenses of 21, 28, 50, 90, 180 and 400 mm. For close-ups I use the Micro-Nikkor 55-mm lens. For reduction of reflections and glare I use a polarizing filter, but otherwise seldom use a filter. I believe that the photographer should work with a minimum amount of equipment and that the camera should be an extension of the eye.

NOTES ON THE PLATES

cover: These clouds were taken looking up from the desert in Arizona. The bright red sunset pigmented the sky, becoming a visual expression of poetry. The photograph speaks for itself, a declaration of emotion.

page 7: This Icelandic geyser intermittently projects jets of water and steam upward. As there is no absolute light there is no absolute color, and the prevailing mood is one of diffuse energy.

page 9: Photographing flowers is always a delight. Their shapes and colors offer infinite possibilities of composition. This snapdragon was taken at a friend's house in Easthampton, Long Island, early on a quiet summer morning.

page 11: The language of color surpasses logic. The artist today is unrestrained by convention in his quest for beauty and truth. This carnival scene at the Seattle World's Fair was taken in the 1960s. Night lights and a long exposure give it a festive surrealistic quality.

page 13: Soft clouds with the hint of the sun in San Francisco at sundown. The ever-changing patterns of clouds have been a subject which continually fascinates me.

page 15: To emphasize the feeling of rain I used a slow shutter speed which enabled me to focus on the blossoms and allow the raindrops to streak across the entire picture. Taken in Tanzania.

page 17: This moody and foreboding picture was taken in Africa at night when I was on assignment on an oil field.

page 21: The photographer finds poetry in reality by constructing a visual experience through the camera's lens. The visual experience, heightened by imagination, creates a truthful illusion. I made several exposures on the same frame, each from a different angle, by moving the camera up and down.

page 25: The prosaic garden reed achieves a sculptural strength and magnitude by making the most of the pre-existing light and shadows. A sense of depth is created by focusing on the outer leaves.

page 27: I used a slow shutter speed to stop the water's action, thereby establishing the feeling of motion. This fresh water stream is in California, and its special shimmering light creates a pattern of icy graffiti.

page 29: The autumn light has its own special quality. I took this picture in Connecticut in the fleeting moment of a freshly fallen leaf.

page 31: The human figure is, to me, a challenging subject. It is only lately that I have had more time to photograph it and experiment with its pure forms. This picture was taken in Monterey, California, in 1978 after three days of photographing the model.

page 33: New England autumn colors are unique in their brightness and hues. This was taken in Connecticut with a wide-angle lens. The golden rays of the sun filter through the tree and onto the newly fallen leaves, capturing a magic moment of color and pattern.

page 35: Soft, misty blue clouds seen through the window of an airplane on one of my frequent cross-country trips from New York to California.

page 39: Water ripples on the Colorado River with selective slivers of light dancing over them. Taken while on assignment to photograph the Grand Canyon. The pattern of ripples create a subjective order in a chaotic world.

page 43: The mother-of-pearl surface on the abalone shell produces infinite variations in color and shape. The change of light can alter the colors and reflections drastically, suggesting an immense vista to the eyes.

page 45: This is a close-up of a "butter lamp" made out of Yak butter, taken in Ladakh, India. The lamp is used for light and in ceremonies.

page 47: The island of Surtsey, near Iceland, was born in 1965. Its crater then boiled and brewed at an incredible temperature, and there was just enough light to outline the background and enable me to capture the red heat of the flowing lava.

page 49: In Palm Springs, California, on a very clear evening when the sky was illuminated by unseen stars, the cross and the moon seemed to be closely related.

page 51: An ancient city seen with a contemporary eye. Shimmering columns of reflected color contrast sharply with the permanency of the black stakes in the water.

page 53: A view of Park Avenue at Christmas time taken from a New York City skyscraper.

page 57: Furrowed ripples from the wake of a ship in a Norway fjord.

page 61: Torches illuminate the streets of Bonn, Germany, with an unearthly glow on the annual Shrove Tuesday witches' parade. An eerie scene.

page 63: A rainbow over the Pinacate Desert in New Mexico in all of its majestic splendor. I photographed this vast desert's geological formations and its flora for about a week and was rewarded by the rainbow's dramatic appearance.

page 66: I found this chunk of uncut glass in a shop in Maine. Its prisms cast infinite reflections of changing light.

page 69: I found these green leaves on a Caribbean island strongly backlighted by the sun, thus creating a definitive white outline.

page 73: Roses are among my favorite flowers to photograph. I took this rose in my studio using the natural light coming in through the window.

page 75: The late afternoon sun of New Mexico with just a few seconds of glow remaining creates the pencil-thin light of the tracks. The Santa Fe railroad's pinhead of light can be seen in the black distance and a lonely telephone pole silhouetted against a dying sky each describe the remarkable drama of light at the day's end.

page 77: Early morning dew in Maine. Many times I shoot for composition, not the subject.

page 79: New York City has an atmosphere of excitement and motion. Here store signs reflect on the wet pavement after a heavy rainfall.

page 81: Taken during a photographic assignment at Yellowstone National Park in winter. The steam of the sulphur and the shadow of the leafless trees suggest a primeval landscape uninhabited by man.

page 83: The deep orange-red colors of a dying sun over this Monterey beach silhouette a bird in flight and outline the lone wading bird searching for his evening meal. Near a friend's house which I often visit.

page 87: I took this picture in Monterey from the ground looking out into the ocean: the funnellike quality of the clouds reflecting the ocean's surface.

page 91: A picture taken in a special moment of leisure in California.

page 93: Inside a temple in Bodhgaya, India, a lone man meditates to the accompaniment of the flickering candles. The soft glow of light imparts a mood of peace and serenity.

page 95: Elephants from the Ringling Brothers Barnum and Bailey Circus taken at the old Madison Square Garden many years ago. I took this with available light using a longer exposure.

page 97: San Francisco's Golden Gate Bridge looms with a ghostly presence as a dramatic background to the startling configuration of car lights. Taken with a slow shutter speed from a car.

page 99: I photographed this snow-covered pine tree while strolling in a park in Luzerne. The tree is decorated by winter's icy fingers with delicate patterns of frosted snow. A fantasy which captures winter's essence.

page 101: A trio of blue flowers with the lens focused on the foreground. I think of a picture as the expression of an impression; and in the creation of the color image we discover the fleeting and transitory nature of color and light.

page 105: The moon poised over the Alps suggests the unearthly quality of an unknown planet. The absolute color of the mountain does not exist. Colors change according to the light in nature as well as exposure.

page 108: In Alberta, Canada, the calm waters reflect the last rays of the intense sunset. Colors not only originate from the breaking down of light, but are also dependent upon it. Too much light, as too little, can destroy color. It is a miraculous relationship.

GOETHE'S LAST WORDS

''More light!''